THANK GOD I'M MANIC

Assorted essays and sketches
by
Rosemary Wren

Rosemary Wren

Rosemary Wren Productions
Santa Cruz, California

ISBN # 0-9635408-0-7

Rosemary Wren Productions
PO Box 8502
Santa Cruz, CA 95061

CONTENTS

✿ ✿ ✿

1. AT YOUR SERVICE

I just got back from Washington. I'm thinking of running for the Senate in a few years so I decided to check it out to see if I could see any signs of sexual harassment. Because if there *is* any sexual harassment I want to be there. Anyway I was walking down the hall of the Senate building and I got pinched two times. Turns out they were testing everyone that day for steroids.

When I got ready to come back to Monterey I had a bright idea. I asked the defense committee if I could borrow a B2 bomber for my trip home. I'm a taxpayer. They said "Oh no, too much gasoline for one person!"

"But if Sununu could, why O why can't I?"

Answer: "He didn't bounce any checks!"

I've always wanted to ride in a B2 — it's such a gorgeous airplane. Did you know that it's run completely by computer and every command is quad-redundant? That means when the pilot pushes the starter those engines get the message four times — pump it up, pump it up. . . But what bothers me is what if the battery dies?

So I chartered a flying saucer instead. Actually I'm glad I didn't ride the B2 home — it had a few bombs still attached, leftovers from the Persian Gulf. My flying saucer landed on top of the Marriott Monterey. They used to have a penthouse up there with a glass roof. Boy, did they get a surprise!

When I got home there was a letter from the power company — 'You have fifteen days to pay your bill or else.' Next day, *next day* they put a notice on the door: 'Unless you pay today before three o'clock we have turned off the lights', signed PG&E.

PG&E favors minus zero population growth. They left the gas on just in case. The only hot things in the house were the water heater and the food in the freezer. I don't think ptomaine poisoning is so bad.

I decided to generate my own electricity but the neighbors complained about toxic waste — the cats located the water fall. I found a few table candles left over from when I used to have company and hoped the charcoal briquets were not hidden too deep in the garage. My garage is dark and gloomy even with the lights on. Luckily the flashlight was in the Earthquake Kit right under the seismic stabilizer, a bottle of champagne. It's a good thing I had to examine that Earthquake Kit as the portable radio was playing *Tower of Power* and just wasting it. At that rate if we had another Big One I wouldn't know what shelter to descend. God works in strange ways to protect the powerless.

No TV. I read and write by flashlight or candles. Abe Lincoln's firelight I haven't tried yet. You know the New York Times Crossword? That goes much better by candlelight — I don't expect so much of myself.

PG&E keeps writing me letters to visit their office or visit the Salvation Army, I think for soup since I can't use the stove. I might visit PG&E office one of these days and take them my latest invention, a generator powered by battery. Also one powered by splitting squash seeds that may replace Mt. Diablo some day. We'd all be a lot happier.

But instead of visiting the power company office I've decided to have them meet me at the corner ice cream shop to discuss my payments. I told them I would be wearing a miner's head lamp which was bought at the Goodwill, be carrying a cold box lunch, and wearing a blinking rose in my lapel. They can't miss me.

The Post Office has its Elvis stamp, the PG&E has its motto. On the back of the envelope it says *At Your Service.* Funeral or electric?

✿ ✿ ✿

2. SNOW WHITE AND THE SEVEN RACCOONS

Things are bad all over. I've been living in a homeless shelter for the past ten days. Only the shelter is my parents' garage. There are no parents on the lot and no house — it went down in the Santa Cruz earthquake of '89. But when my own house in Monterey was foreclosed and sold I headed for spider web heaven to rest my weary heart. Dirt and spiders were not the only problems; it's the story of Snow White and the Seven Raccoons.

Branches from the largest walnut tree in the county rest on the peaked green roof of the ninety year old garage. I haven't had one good night's sleep except for the night I had a cold: I don't think one half bottle of NyQuil is too much. Every night around midnight my sharp-clawed browneyed friends begin climbing the vines and grape arbor onto the roof to play bowling with the walnuts. This continues for hours and just when I think they've called it a night, there they are peering in the window, perched on the arbor. My flashlight on them did not phase, maybe because it shook so much from my pounding heart. The quizzical expression on their faces said — "You're new aren't you?"

When I first became homeless I stayed in various motels. The *InnCal* sign on the highway drew me in, $29.95 for a single — I'm single! *Getting* the room for that price is a different story. Of 100 rooms available only ten are that cheap and they're only for smokers. I would not be upgraded and pay for the pricey winners so my room was next to a pool heater which noised all night long. The next motel rested on Mission Street with huge trucks going by all night. The exception to losers like this is the Motel 6 chain which gives good value for the money, all rooms are the same price and they are open to suggestions for improved service.

Can you believe I headed for the garage even though it has no electricity, running water or you know what! Many of the studio/apartments I looked at to rent were rundown, shabby or you had to go through the carport to get to the bathroom. Some landlords told me "these are OK for the students or hispanics."

The third day in nut heaven my son Chris came from San Francisco to investigate his homeless mother. After breaking into tears we had some good laughs and I talked him into painting the walls and putting on some locks. I had slept (not slept) two nights without security. My nightly nightmares had taken place in a sleeping bag resting on a mattress on the floor. With the cement floor and Santa Cruz night vapors I was coughing a bit. Chris was able to make a platform for the bed from two steamer trunks and a table. Now the air is warmer but it is the exact height of an operating table. I have bad dreams of masked doctors coming toward me in rubber gloves.

I finished painting the walls the other day and I'm beginning to like the daytime. Besides the raccoons at night there is at least one possum. The neighborhood cat had him up a tree yesterday and he leaped from branch to branch yelling his head off and slapping that tail.

I have applied to rent a low-income unit at the new complex up the street. The waiting list is quite long but if you live in sub-standard housing you have a better chance. A home is considered sub-standard if:

- it does not have indoor plumbing
- does not have a flush toilet
- does not have a bathtub/shower
- does not have electricity
- does not have heat
- does not have a kitchen

My garage qualifies on all counts. This federally subsidized housing complex had me take a form to the city building inspector for him to come out and verify I was living in substandard housing. When he saw it he questioned their sanity. If he declares my garage 'unfit' I will have to move immediately and

then be on the street unless the housing comes through. Is this a Catch 22 or what?

I have discovered a delightful Japanese style bath house in town. There I can sit in the hot tub and ponder. It is quiet except for the rustle of bamboo waving in the open garden and an occasional wind chime. The first visit to the bath house I was afraid to stay in the tub too long — too exhausted and faint!

McDonalds, TacoBell and 7-11 are my hot food places and I eat veggies and fruits and lots of walnuts. My face has broken out in acne which I haven't had since a teenager, I have lost weight and have had some dizzy spells.

I try to garden to get my mind off it. There were some rusty garden tools in the garage. I'll be OK until I run out of money. I am lucky. I have a roof over my head (although subject to nightly bombardment), money to buy food, and an overgrown secret garden outside the door. What of those with no shelter or money?

I wept a lot today. It happens especially when I see a homeless person on the street. With knife-sharp pain in my heart and stomach I am still lucky. What of them?

✿ ✿ ✿

3. THANK GOD I'M MANIC

Two years ago a well-known news show had an extended segment on manic-depressive syndrome. While I realize their desire to publicize this so-called disease in order to show its positive aspects, I must as a composer/artist come to the defense of composers, artists, poets, friends who are said to have this condition.

Unlike Handel, Mozart and Mahler, many creative geniuses have never reached their potential nor has the world accepted their gifts. They were not able to rise above the derision, isolation and ostracism which is even more intense in present day society than it was in the 18th and 19th centuries. This ostracism has been enforced by the medical/scientific experts who label exceptionally talented people with bursts of exciting creativity as having manic-depressive illness. I maintain that the downside of these artistic people might be prevented or mollified if they were treated as human beings, recognizing and appreciating their genius and not rejecting them from childhood as subnormal or categorizing them as ill or mentally disordered, a stigma that never leaves.

Referrals to psychiatrists and psychologists by teachers and school authorities because a child is 'different' can be the start of trouble for the genius rather than help. He is immediately set apart and labeled. If the strange behavior begins later in life, may it not be a reaction to what the person has experienced all along? If you are continually treated like you are unacceptable you begin acting more unacceptable than ever, are rejected, and as a result depressed.

The scientific genius is always more valued in our society than the artistic. The constant appetite for high tech, the movement toward technocracy, provides employment, monetary gain and stature to the physicist, the computer whiz, the geneticist. His work is rewarded, he is valued.

The majority of artists, composers and writers can rarely live from their art. They are denied the pleasure to enjoy their creative highs and be rewarded for them. When they have produced that giant by soaring with the angels, when they come back to earth, no one wants their work, no one appreciates it, publishes/buys/performs it, or even cares. When as a result they become depressed or suicidal they are drugged, hospitalized and sometimes given shock treatment. This is an illness? a mental disorder? I think not.

I have been seriously composing music, painting and writing poetry for the past twelve years. Before that I was married, raised a family of four children, and was a music teacher. I once composed the majority of a musical in one weekend. (In a fever.) I have composed two musicals, an opera, a large choral work, and many songs. Only one musical has been produced because I produced it. I have written several books of poetry — no publisher, painted hundreds of paintings and sold a few. Is this depressing?

Yet I get these fevers to create. And I welcome them along with the struggle, pain, isolation. I am not on medication, have never been hospitalized for being an artist. But I have been called 'crazy' and I do get depressed.

When I was a child I experienced simple people with no medical or psychological knowledge who embraced the exceptionals in their midst without intellectualizing them or medicating them away. Their solution was faith, compassion, intuitive understanding and acceptance. There must be a culture somewhere that does this — or did I imagine it in one of my manic highs.

✿ ✿ ✿

4. ROSEMARY'S MONTEREY GARDEN

FOUR ESSAYS

I

Those scrub blue jays are always asking me questions. As soon as I come out the door there they go — who's going to be the next president, why are the Israelites still building condos on the West Bank, and why didn't you water the hydrangeas? Most of the time I love their company as they are a cheerful bunch; but they do have a right to ask.

In California we believe in consensus so I might be able to get some of this on the ballot to see what flys. The only proposition which hasn't made it to the voters is do we still approve Diablo Canyon.

Our island in the sun did break away from the continental mass during the earthquake. It was long overdue and had been predicted by Jeanette McDonald when she sang 'San Francisco, Open your Golden Gate'. Fortunately the union of the United States still claims it. The value of owning an island was clearly demonstrated by the war over the Falklands between Britain and Argentina; and bougainvillea, orchids and gardenias do a lot better when surrounded by water.

I thought of moving to beautiful, quiet Dolores, Colorado where I know some people.

Rosmary
© 1990

It is a small town with a lot of altitude. I would miss the California exciting strange things not only the earthquakes. Also drought, freeze, tanker-shipped water from Alaska, lettuce at eight-nine cents a head, and the inquisitive blue jays in my garden.

The scrub blue jay lifestyle is different than mine their economy being more assured. They are always showing me struggling insects and fat juicy worms held in their beaks. They feast richly on garden seeds, holly berries and constantly sneak bright red kernels from the asparagus 'Sprengeri' fern.

I think they answered their first question about the presidential election themselves. 'We are ready for a domestic president who will protect our habitat in the camellia bushes.' One who negotiated a settlement between a group of homeowners who didn't want to have their homes condemned so a high school could be constructed on the land. This was a tough one. Without forsaking the needy and the environment, this governor balanced the budget when he first took office in his home state. (It was not Arkansas.) Nine years later he is working to balance the budget in his state and having a difficult time. He has not done a lot on the foreign scene but he can settle fights.

On the other hand the incumbent, who travels a lot, had enough influence on the Israelites to get them to the peace table. When you think of the Battle of Jericho and the battle against the Philistines, you are thinking formidable and tenacious spirit. Think also that roses grew on the coastal plane of Sharon and lilys in King Solomon's garden. That from the first to the fifth centuries AD wine from Carmel by the Sea (Mediterranean) was famous; that the plains of Jericho were covered with rare and precious balsam plantations when the Romans entered Palestine around 63 B.C.

The answer to the third question about why I don't water the hydrangeas is that we don't have a dam.

In the early 1960s several Sicilian villages were parched and poverty stricken, much drier than my Monterey garden. There was no water for the crops, people were starving, and the dams promised by the government were mysteriously slow to materialize. In Sicily the people say 'Water is another God'.

Over a period of nine years the famous Italian political activist, Danilo Dolci, had fasted seven times to protest the inaction of the government, the political resistance of the Mafia and the apathy of the Catholic Church toward the building of two dams.

By 1963 Dolci's efforts in fasting and organization paid off for the dam on the Iato River. The remaining dam to be built was Bruca on the Belice River behind the village of Roccamena. The Bruca dam had been projected since 1930 with no action. Danilo Dolci grasped the situation with both hands. He started a ten day fast and sympathy fasts began by the town's people and other groups all over Europe. The ninth day of the fast the whole village walked a protest march four miles to the dam site and by the tenth day the government pledged to build the Bruca Dam.

Shall we gather at the river?

✿ ✿ ✿

II

Acacia trees are volunteering in the driveway cracks. Since this is a supreme act of courage I hate to pull them up. I notice things like this because the television set is broken. Black-eyed Susans are also making an attempt in the driveway; the purple flowered potato vine (just back from the freeze) is climbing Marina rose bush, and Seashell roses turn from peach to pink once they're in the house for three days. There are four kinds of weeds in the lawn and raccoons do not replace their divots. I miss *Moneyline* and *Auto Racing*.

One thing I have not seen here is the Mediterranean Fruit Fly. Maybe it's because I have only one fruit tree, a Santa Rosa Plum, which bore about seventy-five delicious plums a year and half after planting. In the early eighties when California was threatening to spray malathion from airplanes on orchards in the Santa Clara valley, I invited relatives from that area to come and stay with me during the spraying period. If Monterey is ever threatened by malathion I'll be leaving for Abbu Dabbi.

Some people look good when they garden. The proper apron or smock has pockets and loops for all the various tools, their hats are attractive straw from Panama, their feet in colorful clogs, and they have foam rubber knee cushions covered in bright canvas. Every once in awhile I catch a glimpse of myself in the window when I'm gardening and it is frightening: antique Pebble Beach golf cap, dowdy shorts with turtle neck shirt, and tennis shoes at least ten years old, slick on the bottom. This can make it dangerous on a hilly slope where pine needles act as skis, or on wet grass when you wrench your back. My weeding cushion is a blue chintz sofa pillow — faded. Tennis and golf are much more fashionable to say nothing of Jazzercise.

I miss *Wall Street Week* and *Kamikaze* but the pink Queen Elizabeth climber on the front of the house has chosen the month of November to bloom for the first time in two years. There's that morning light through the Monterey pines and blue jays splashing in the fountain. Camellia petals floating in the birdbath or glowing on a pile of clippings in the rain are the force that turns the world. How lucky I am to observe up close a small section of its crust.

One life to live.

✿ ✿ ✿

III

I have some of the only plants in Monterey County to reject homemade compost. It may be because the pine needles did not decompose while the clippings, cabbage and apple cores did. Although I have millions of pine needles on my property I will not use them to make compost again. They can rot on their own. However, I must say that the plants who liked the compost truly shot out of the ground and came in colors that put neon to shame — plus green how I love you green!

In conversations with gardens I always assure them that I have their best interests at heart. They don't always cooperate because they know I'm just starting. Like how I told those brilliant orange flowers not to jump on the sidewalk. But a week later they did and strangled my adorable lavender Campanula muralis to death. The next time I talked to them in Italian, this being Monterey, and they did better.

That coral geranium by the front door has wild parties for cut worms which put me at a great disadvantage. I am an organic gardener and will not kill. We had a talk about this and I threatened to dig him up and give him to my neighbor. One morning after three warnings I was ready with the shovel, only to find no worms. I think they jumped the sidewalk.

We are all late bloomers and I wish we would hurry up. I do get a lot of advice 'cause I ask for it. Acid for creatures in California sounds risky — who am I to contradict? Not sugar cubes, but shiny azure blue crystals that you dissolve in water were supposed to change my yellow-leafed camellias to verdant green with a shot of iron to boost. After the first application the leaves turned from chartreuse to curry yellow. (Yes, I followed the directions.) Next month, mustard shade, and after a suitable interval and more dilution than called for, the leaves were just plain brown. I blamed myself, stood on the fertilizer box and lectured in the middle of the garden and went to the library. Mystery. Well, acid trips are illegal.

Organics have a hard time. I thought my father was way off base when he put spagetti way back in his Santa Cruz garden to distract the ants from the house. Now I don't think so. I'll try anything including compost made with chow mein. I have seen documentaries on the fields in China and they are light years ahead. How anyone could revolt against that is beyond me.

My son's girlfriend Joanne gave me a charming gift — a picturesque tin full of regional wild flower seeds. Only the region is Texas. Plains coreopsis, Mexican hat, Missouri evening primrose, Wild Bergamot, Texas Bluebonnet, Firewheel. Whoopee! Spring don't be late! They are peeping up through the Monterey soil and I'm hoping for a little bit of Texas in my back yard. I will charge admission to see them. I think this might be the "Houston Solution"† to my garden, but please, no Lone Star Poison Oak because I am just recovering from California!

In spite of all this I'm so delirious in the garden that I sometimes burst into song. It's OK with the plants. But the neighbor always leaves with slamming doors and squealing tires. This ostentatious exit also occurs when I practice violin in the living room with the windows open.

The other day when walking past the lime shrub I distinctly hear a voice: "I'm choking! I'm choking!" When I parted the leaves, sure enough there was an iron collar around her neck attached to the fence by wires. I had been wondering about her pale visage and quickly removed her choker. After that she did so well for two weeks, new leaves and all and four tiny limes. Now she has curly leaf aphids. Maybe I can distract them with some spagetti.

† Country Western song

IV

GARDEN CRISIS IN THE GULF

Plants are not themselves these days and it could be the crisis in the gulf. The shrubs who know they are drought resistant are *not* resisting. We must remember that our global ecosystem is connected. When Saddam Hussein decided to change things there was a definite reaction in my garden. However the message I got from the loquat trees, with their yellowing leaves, was — don't send troops from California. They are needed here to fight fires.

Things look rather sad and droopy — the calla lillies lay down on the ground as soon as they're born. They are not marching to the war drums. The wild flowers have all ready given up for the summer, and they were supposed to tolerate 'no water.' They all seem bloody bored by the whole scene in the desert and at the rate the reserves are drinking bottled water, we may well be dry again next year. It makes me thirsty.

It is like a grade B movie and I'm against sending the boys 'over there'. You don't have to go to Arabia to have maneuvers in the sand

— California this year is pretty much mega desert and you wouldn't be interfering in someone else's business. I thought we joined the United Nations a long time ago to participate not jump-start aggression.

The Monterey Pine trees pretend to play golf so all is well. There are a few brave roses here and there but what they tell me every morning is: we need water, not oil.

✿ ✿ ✿

5. I LOVE CHOLESTEROL

I can eat mashed potatoes with butter — they soothe my tummy and my psyche. When every trip to the mail box means nobody wants my stories, music or paintings, when I can't get that loan, when the phone never rings — I mash hot potatoes with milk and drizzle with salt, pepper and melted butter. Oh yes. Or if it's middle morning, get the car out of the garage and drive to Reds Doughnuts for two of their delish glazed ones.

Baker's Square is my idea of an affirmative restaurant. In Salinas I went there to dine on my way to the theatre. I sat and sat and all the waitresses glanced my way from afar for ten minutes. I told the manager. I told the manager and my salad and sandwich came rushing like lightning, served by the hostess herself. The manager followed with coffee. But the 'coup de maitre' was they invited me for dessert on the house because of the delay. I couldn't accept 'cause I was too full. But they insisted on a huge piece of lemon meringue pie packed in a box for later. Yes!

The other day my doctor said my cholesterol was high. I explained why. I had just had a plate of bacon and eggs before the test.

And I hate fiber. I do eat broccoli or one or two green things every day. Also a couple of oranges, apples, peaches and cream or similar. It there's fiber there I am not aware. I know I won't eat toast oats and bran squares.

I'm not fat but I'm pleasantly plump — and growing. The latest is ice cream with no cream. Well then they can't call it ice cream — I'm going to sue. Shoppers have to be stubborn as a diet drink and have radar eyes to spot the real stuff. I have brought home 'frozen light', imitation vanilla and tutti-fruti yogurt which all gave me pains in my stomach and terrible indigestion. Now I spend at least twenty minutes reading every subtitle. Decent cream is being replaced by double six HIO and I'm dying for Bordens Creamery when I was eight and thick chocolate milk shakes took care of your appetite for a couple of hours at least.

It is very strange that in wartime cholesterol was OK to eat. In fact it was so desirable that meat, eggs, cheese and butter had to be rationed so that everyone got enough. To those American dietitians, faddists, and doctors nowadays who don't want their butter, eggs and cream, send them to Russia! They are standing in line for commodities and would appreciate your 'genrous-troika'.

In one of the soup kitchens where I was a volunteer waitress we were not allowed to give seconds on dessert. The dietitian said rich food and sugar were too stimulating for the homeless, especially if they were mentally ill. I used to sneak them pastries or whatever was available and it always stimulated them — to smile!

I don't know how my parents ever survived to be long-lived senior citizens. They ate well balanced old-fashioned meals including frequent breakfasts of linguica and eggs, fried potatoes, biscuits and sliced fresh peaches from their Santa Cruz garden.

If nobody wants to publish this article I won't go out in the garden and eat worms — unless they're made out of butter and sugar. I know what I'll do. That night for dinner I'll have mashed potatoes, fried chicken, fresh green beans, Waldorf salad and tapioca pudding for dessert. Yes, yes, yes and whoopee!

✿ ✿ ✿

6. THE SANTA MONICA STATE OF MIND

SAV-RITE
MUSKRAT
Vintage
CLOTHING
Rosemary Wren
© 1990

Night. I have just seen a glitz-slick movie at gorgeous new clean AMC theatre on gorgeous new clean jacaranda Third Street Promenade. The street was mass people at the *Festa D'Italia.* But I am three blocks from the crowd and it's dark quiet and my car won't start. It's old. So I sit there and am not afraid. I have been in Santa Monica three days but I know it: broad streets, some traffic, delicious fog, friendly people. Friendly people? That morning the bank teller at World Savings told me 'There are only ten nice ones in LA!' I guess I met them. The car finally starts.

LA seems older than upstate and grew faster and the streets are dirtier. I used to feel Northern California girl superior to the South before I lived awhile in New York City. Now I get the connection. In a young country New York is ancient buildings, gray streets, old trees, litter, pulse and rush. In a young state LA is older cubes of concrete, pop artytecture, ugly and great mid-rises, litter, pulse and rush, and not enough trees. LA basin can bloom in green and help balance out the smog. Trees, trees trees. I drove on Wilshire for blocks without seeing one. Long gray streets can be lined in trees worth their weight in leaves that screen the air. It's a start!

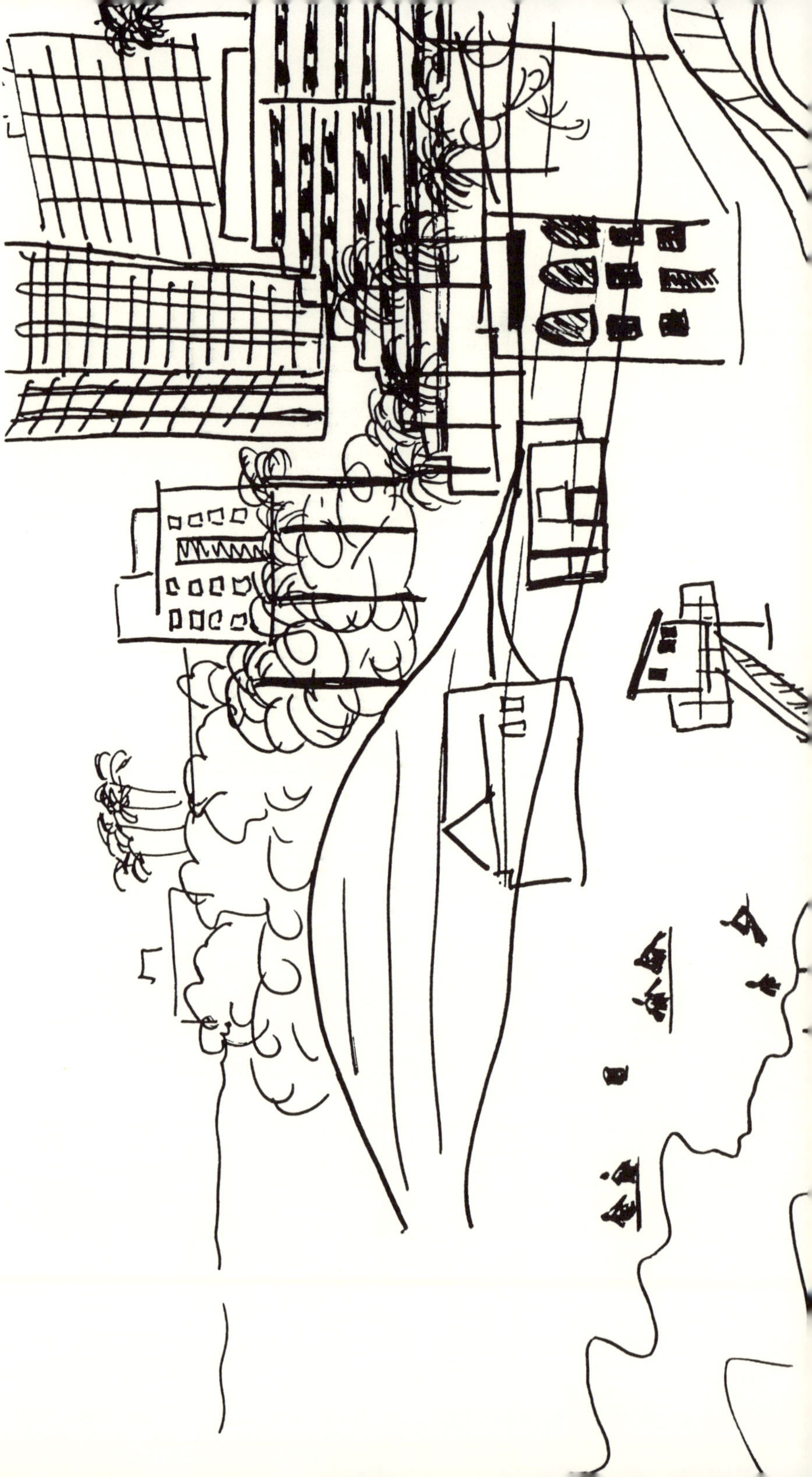

Which brings me back to Santa Monica. It was humid, hot. The Jacaranda trees spread lavender snows even downtown. They border the new Third Street Promenade and are most shocking when you catch a quick purple-blue sight elsewhere in the city. Entering a magnolia street north of Wilshire was cool and tunnely, a sweet breath — deep green leaves and velvet white flowers. Magnolia trees for downtown LA? Well maybe not. But how about Portugal Laurel, a shiny evergreen umbrella tree. Or White Peppermint Eucalyptus, a well-mannered street tree, dark green dense foliage, light trunk, twenty to fifty feet, white flowers.

Santa Monica cares — the street people don't want to leave. It soothes their broken hearts more than any other place. The city has great social programs for the homeless but there are those who don't want social homes. They feel out of pulse, rejected. Ragged clothes and souls they sit looking out of glazed eyes into the sea.

In LA every commercial establishment is compelled to fill my ears with music I don't want to hear. From Thrifty Drugs to a trendy restaurant on Montana Avenue it was the same boring sound. There I complained. It was changed from 'easy listenin' to Vivaldi. The sounds of the city, somebody's words, your own still small voice are all blocked out.

PALM
MOTEL
© 1990

In Santa Monica Michael Jackson was a few blocks away at St. Johns Hospital — chest pains. They couldn't figure out why he was ailing because he doesn't smoke, drink or eat junk food. That's it! No junk food. The man needs something to stick to his ribs like meat and potatoes — some ribs and sweet potato pie once in a while to keep his ribs in shape. I thought of visiting him to cheer him up. But his suite cost thousands and I was staying at the Palm Motel.

The Palm Motel is one of the most downright LA 30s Raymond Chandler historicals around. Big old palm trees and garages! Painted clean but no frills homey, red tile roofs, window box geraniums and neon signs, it has flags of many countries painted on its walls. This is to make international guests feel at home; the Palms is listed in the European budget motel directory. And the palms do sing in the night, cars come and go, and the homeless who sit on the front doorstep all night are allowed to drink the free coffee.

Friday morning I sat and sketched the Santa Monica Carousel. A slight, wrinkled grayhaired lady wandered tentatively in, vulnerable face. She startled when I said hello. She was so alone I wanted to hug her, hold her, tell her I understood. We did not speak but I know her.

Later when I saw her crossing the bridge I recognized that lonely, jerky walk.

Some lonely people go to the library a lot — they can be alone yet in company. I always go to the library especially in a new town. It gives me a feel for the city. Santa Monica's huge white 60s library was busy with people of all ages on my first day in LA. The clerks didn't mind leaving their computers to give me maps and directions.

Directions to Venice to hear mystery writer Rochelle Krich read from her first book. These readings happen every week or so in the Mystery Annex of *Small Books Bookstore* on the beach. Directions to West LA College to hear their jazz band play 'Oldies and Goodies'. And later in the week to hear the Santa Monica College Chorale sing Britten and Verdi. That concert ended with a Jongen Organ Concerto played by Catharine Crozier and the Los Angeles Concert Orchestra that blew the roof off the Methodist church.

I'm still a little afraid of the freeways but once my shaky Ford hit the San Diego Freeway it caught the rhythm, not criss-crossing lanes or anything that close, but knowing its own mind and making the true and right exits with all the other old LA cars, and there are a few.

I like that LA pulse — I can feel it on the Santa Monica Pier or way up Wilshire, in poetry readings at Duttons Brentwood, shabby-down blocks in Venice, thumping in the freeway, throbbing light out of Hollywood Hills, in musical hispanic voices and the night singing palms of Santa Monica — where I seem to begin the LA state of mind.

✿ ✿ ✿

7. MANHATTAN JEWEL: FORT TRYON PARK

The snow lighted our way as it fell softly on shoulders and pricked our faces. We were walking toward the Cloisters in the dreamlike mist of a winter morning in Ft. Tryon Park. It could have been more than three hundred years ago when the Wiechquasesgeck Indians still occupied the territory — the snow had practically hidden the vestiges of the 20th century. We were in another world, ethereal and almost spiritual in the intensity of its beauty.

The charm of this setting would stand alone without the Cloisters, the medieval branch of the Metropolitan Museum within the park; but they complement each other. This same winter day I caught my breath when I entered a room in the Cloisters — there in the center was a magnificent flower bed of pure white: crocus, tulips, cyclamen. Not much else adorned the gray stony interior of that room except when one looked out the arched windows the snowscape echoed the brilliance of the flowers.

My July walk in the park was quite a contrast to winter. I was accompanied by Perry Rasero, a landscape gardener from the New York City Parks Department, who provided the proper names for some of the sixteen hundred species of trees, shrubs and plants flourishing in the soft almost tropical air. In fact overgrowth is now one of the big problems in the park, obscuring views and preventing definition of plantings. The resulting lush greenery is wild and appealing on the hilly terrain.

The Promenade where we began our walk is lined with Elm trees backed by such beautys as Norway Maple, Dogwood, Mulberry, Ginko and an occasional Copper Beech. The path closest to the Hudson is alive with marigolds, petunias, johnny-jump-ups, veronicas, phlox and geraniums. Patches of coral day lilys spread below the main terrace; a magnificent white hydrangea climbs the north bank and purple trumpet vines cover the arches.

Ft. Tryon Park is the unsung treasure of Manhattan Island, partly because it is at the very north of the island, and because Central Park o'ershadows it in publicity and location. Aficionados of the Hudson know the park for its sweeping views of that river from terraces and plateaus, walks and knolls. And many Washington Heights residents stroll the Promenade bordered with benches where one can sit in relative quiet and watch the passing scene. In fact Frederick Law Olmsted Jr., principal designer of the park, planned paths, benches and terraces at many levels where people could stroll and sit uncrowded, almost in solitude if desired. Each stopping place was designed to present a view of the Hudson or the city in a different framework 'some intricate and intimate, some grandiose and simple, and some gardenesque or naturalistic', in Olmsted's words.

The Olmsted brothers whose parent firm designed Central Park, carried on the 'eighteenth century English naturalistic romantic tradition' in Ft. Tryon Park: small open lawns, wooded slopes, views of the Hudson and Palisades, and random gardens.

During the 19th century the land was occupied by the private estates of prominent people — Billings, Libbey, Chittenden, Watkins. But it was an 18th century woman, Margaret Cochran Corbin, who left the most intriguing story. One of the fiercest battles of the Revolutionary War took place on Forest Hill later to be called Ft. Tryon by the British. In the heat of that battle Mrs. Corbin helped her husband, John, by loading the cannon until he was killed, then taking his place until she was wounded and captured. The entrance to the park Corbin Circle is named for her.

The fiftieth anniversary of Ft. Tryon Park was celebrated in 1985 — fifty years of beauty made possible by a gift from John D. Rockefeller Jr. In 1935 the official dedication was attended by Mayor LaGuardia, Park Commissioner Robert Moses, General Hugh S.

Rosemary Wren
© 1992

Johnson of the WPA, and George Blumenthal, President of the Metropolitan Museum.

Mr. Rockefeller said in his presentation: 'And now, as my dream is about to be realized, I am hoping two things. First that this spot, whose natural beauty has only been enhanced by the hand of man, may in the years to come bring as great happiness to you, the people of New York, as it has brought to me during the many years that have passed. Secondly, that you will cherish and preserve it with the same brooding care and untiring interest which have made it what it is today.'

Rockefeller had been struck by the indefinable quality of this site — he acquired the parcel and kept it for twenty years until his dream could come true. He too may have walked the magic walk in the snow or stood overlooking the Hudson in the cool fragrance of a summer morning.

Although the park is neglected from lack of funds and mistreated by those who do not realize its treasure, there are many who work hard to restore and maintain Rockefeller's dream. The *Friends of Ft. Tryon Park* started in 1983 by Carol Weinstein, is one group who weed, clean and plant on a regular basis. They can be seen on weekends working at Corbin Circle, along the Promenade, around the gazebo, in the apple orchard and the grounds of the Cafe. They also sponsor brisk morning walks thru the park on weekdays at six AM!

Ms. Weinstein started the group as a result of her frequent shopping trips from Washington Heights thru the park to Broadway. One day she came across an abandoned car on one of the main paths to the Cloisters. Every day for a week there it was — until one day instead of the car she found a little old lady sweeping up glass with a tree branch. Carol began helping her and several bystanders joined in and the *Friends* began.

These days the Heather Garden and the Promenade were closed until May of 1992 for Phase II of the park's reconstruction. At the Cloisters an amazing series of lectures and workshops go on all year long. *Saturdays at the Cloisters* are gallery talks; 'Knights, Weapons and Valor', 'Medieval Heraldry', and 'Tapestry Weaving ' are lecture titles from a recent calendar. Every month Family Gallery workshops are held for children ages 4-12 and their families on subjects such as 'Heroines, Queens and Ladies'.

Six acres of the sixty-seven acre Ft. Tryon Park are being rebuilt. There will be reconstruction of pathways, drainage systems, benches and landscaping. This was John D. Rockefeller's dream and greatest hope: that Manhattan's jewel, Ft. Tryon Park, would inspire the community to help with its maintenance and preservation. That the wondrous walks, heather gardens, quiet benches and magnificent views would balance the mighty city towers and the rush of the crowds.

✿ ✿ ✿

UPPER MANHATTAN

No island could be more exotic
The pastoral sky of Dutch settlers
heavy with farmland purity
returns every autumn morning
over the Hudson
to sit on George Washington Bridge
to send pink codes off silver towers
Helicopters and airplanes answer
with drones, hums and static clacks
swooping toward the river
gliding into nothing
into the mainstream of the universe
toward Asia and Russia
or back to the airport

There must be a huge lamp
in the depths
of the Hudson River
It sends diffuse rays
which only break into light
as they reach the surface
There they swiftly shop the shadows
or ride the train
of a tugboat's wake

In winter there are fewer barges
scattering the ice with definite purpose
as we on the island watch with envy
their easy float
going somewhere through the gray
This is also a time
when the sky is pure
having dropped its veils of snow
in wind swells off the Hudson

And sometimes in winter we watch
the dawn moving in on the bridge
and once again
pink codes are sent off silver towers
The birds in Fort Tryon Park
answer with chirps and song
They have remained

✿ ✿ ✿

8. DESIGN, WOMAN, DESIGN

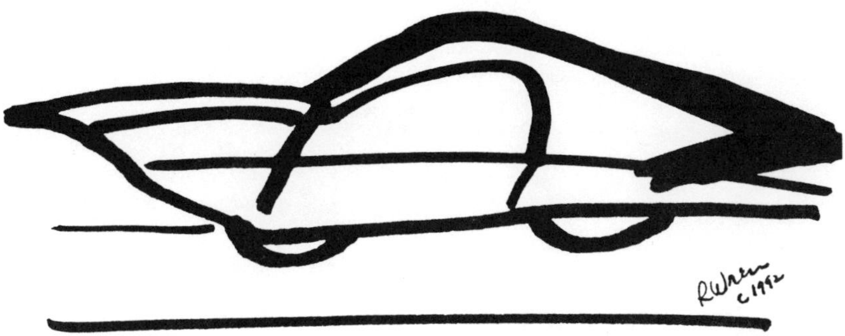

American women should do more of the designing in this world. The Hubble Space Telescope should have been designed by a woman — can you imagine her putting in a defective mirror? And the Space Shuttle Columbia has been leaking hydrogen. Women don't pack lunch boxes with leaky thermoses; they stand at the sink and test them up and down, up and down . . .

As for the B2 Stealth Bomber I cannot quarrel with its design. It is the most beautiful airplane I have ever seen! However I would convert it to a peacetime aircraft, preferrably passenger. Currently it is a two seater for two pilots. I would design a series of sleek skylights instead of passenger windows. But there are a couple of things about the B2 that have me worried: apparently each pilot has a stick that sets all sorts of computerized electronic things in motion and the answer to each of his commands is 'quad-redundant'. What bothers me is if the battery dies. Engineers believe that recent computer problems on the Magellan were caused by a cosmic ray during the observation of Venus. How romantic! The only way I can relate is when I go to the library or bank and stand in line forever because the computer is down.

The B2 has an interesting way of cooling its jets. Some cleverly designed doors on both sides of the nacelles (engine enclosures) open to ventilate the motors. The doors are so streamlined they barely make a ripple in the 172 foot wingspan. I live in hope to actually see this gorgeous bird and would know I was in heaven to fly in it. Meanwhile, pictures.

Streamlined may be a cliché but the B2 puts new meaning on the word. It is time for a woman to step forward and do for the automotive industry what Northrup designers have done for aviation. Boxes on wheels with baggage compartments on their backs are the sedans of the eighties, hopefully not the nineties, as the bustle went out a long time ago. Automobiles all look alike from haute couture to volksy peasant so why wait for a better rebate? We are ready for the kind of design that produced the Studebaker of the forties, the Thunderbird of the fifties or the fishtail Cadillac. Unique!

High rises with blank stone walls to the street are incompatible with the feminine psyche. She wants to window shop to see what's there before entering. There is a weaker sex instinct that stops me from visiting cold formidable skyscrapers unless I can see other people coming and going on the ground floor. Those who enter may never return! The architectural ideal of function and involvement with the community is stopped cold by a blank wall at eye level.

In a 1985 directory of designers who have created milestones and set the pace, only twenty women out of 339 designers are listed. The majority of these twenty are in the fields of furniture, fashion, textile and interior design and only one woman is American. The book is a guide to well-designed consumer goods and its designers from the last 100 years. The selection was made by a British designer, Terence Conran which may explain its emphasis on the British and Europeans.(1)

The United States has a comparatively young history of design. The 19th century tendency in the US to look to Europe for culture, art and 'good design' persisted into the first two decades of the 20th. During the Depression the industrial design profession emerged to meet the needs of mass production in the machine age. Products of this time were Teague's plastic Kodak and the standard Bell telephone.

A recent book (1988) NEW AMERICAN DESIGN presents twenty-one of America's leading young industrial and graphic design firms and their products. Most of the designers are in their thirties and started their businesses during the last ten years. Of the 115 designers thirty-three are women.(2)

A definition of American design at this point is complex. Design is form is function is symbol is cultural icon is esthetic media is derivative is . . . . Graphic designers in the US are rebelling against traditional European precedents and are striving in some cases for anti-mechanical imperfection, fragmentation, intuitive, humanistic and shocking methods. Hidden meanings and puzzling juxtaposition require the viewer to spend some time exploring. This young radical spirit is commendable and has its place as an art form. But if a poster is to inform quickly it should be legible and understood and also well designed. One does not always have time to stand deciphering abstract graphics in a shop window or when leafing through a newspaper.

What is important is that there seems to be a body of American design in formation, highly individual yet drawing on the rich heritage of the country. Women are sure to enter such an exciting field.

frogdesign, a German firm based in the Silicone Valley calls the rounded edges of its Apple Computer 'female design'; they say 'female design' adds emotional appeal to technological products. We know that! It's female *designers* who can add richness and beauty to industrial design and at the same time include proper mirrors. Streamlined is here to stay!

(1) *The Conran Directory of Design* Ed. Stephen Bayley Villard Books NY 1985

(2) *New American Design* Hugh Aldersey-Williams Rizzoli NY 1988

✿ ✿ ✿

9. TED AND GLORIA AND THE PANCULTURAL ORCHESTRA

I hadn't touched the violin for over thirty years but when Maestro Gargiulo raised the baton I did start playing with everyone else. As the sound poured forth including my wrong notes, I choked up and tears blinded my eyes. To be making music with other people, other instruments — I was not prepared for the thrill of it! I suddenly realized how much I had missed playing with an orchestra. Since that day I have never missed a rehearsal. (And I practice violin every day.)

The setting for this joyful musical experience is the Defense Language Institute at the Presidio of Monterey: the group is the Pancultural Orchestra composed of students from the language school and people from the Monterey community.

I will soon give you a history of this orchestra but first let me tell you about two special professional people who make it all possible: Theodore Gargiulo, musicologist, veteran conductor of symphony and opera in the U.S. and Canada, and Gloria Gargiulo, his warm, welcoming wife, lyric soprano and artistic director. They provide the atmosphere in which professional and amateur can feel comfortable playing music together. Maestro Gargiulo wants the best from his players — but he can

criticize your mistakes in such a way that you take it as a compliment! He can hear that D flat which should be natural even when it's buried in the loudest sounds.

The romantic New York City circumstance which brought the Gargiulos together was a rehearsal of the *Coro D'Italia*, a community chorus featuring Italian folk songs, dances and operatic repertoire. Ted was the conductor/composer in residence; Gloria, lyric soprano was a soloist. For love of the chorus, opera stars such as Licia Albanese and basso Giorgio Tozzi appeared with the group in annual concert.

One of the advantages to being a music student in New York City was the chance to observe the "greats" in action and to learn from them. Both Gloria and Ted proclaim this as a very important part of their musical education. Young Gloria worked at Tiffany's, sang all the time in opera, concerts, week-end club dates and attended New York University to study languages and business. She also went to the Metropolitan Opera every Friday night to glean from the singers. Ted credits his conducting skill to observing Toscanini, Beecham, Mitropoulos, and playing bass clarinet under the baton of Stokowski in the National Youth Administration symphony. His formal training in harmony, theory and orchestration was scholarship study at the Manhattan School of

Music, New York Philharmonic Symphony Society and with Fritz Stiedry of the Metropolitan Opera.

Peninsula violinist Rebecca Sulavik says: "Ted is a gentleman and a conductor who is easy to work with. He gives individual attention. As a new-comer to the area I joined the orchestra because I love music and love playing with others."

Music, music, music led the Gargiulos and their children Franca and Terrence to the Monterey Peninsula in 1972 when Ted came to Ft. Ord to be Director of Music for Morale Support Services. The journey from New York had included opera conducting in Miami, Washington DC and Cleveland, as well as tours in the U.S. and Canada. On his way to leading the Pancultural Orchestra, Ted conducted one very similar in nature. The Columbus Symphony in Georgia where the couple lived for seven years was composed of lawyers, doctors, high school students, paid professionals and others from the community.

The DLI Pancultural Orchestra was the dream of Rabbi (Col.) Seymour Moskowitz, who established it in 1984. Ardent supporter Moskowitz used to sit beaming through every rehearsal and was a constant friend of the group. The DLI Comandant at the time Col.

David A. McNerney, felt it was truly appropriate for a language school to have an orchestra since "music is the international language par excellance!"

The present Chaplain, (Major) John Babcock, instructor in World Religions and Cultures, explained that the orchestra furthers cultural expression since it plays music from many countries.

Chaplain Babcock says "The orchestra gives students a change of pace, a break from their constant study, an opportunity for artistic expression." Unfortunately the military does not furnish instruments as they are not a budgeted item. Large instruments are loaned by local schools and bands.

How about missles into tubas? A few weeks ago I met a young DLI student who came to rehearsal but couldn't play because she didn't have a flute. She had just arrived on post and was hoping to join the orchestra. I never saw her at rehearsal again.

Happily for percussionist Pvt. Joseph Kuhlman who arrived from Quincy, Ill. in August to study German, there was a timpani. (A little hard to carry on your back from Illinois!) Pvt. Kuhlman says: "I played percussion all through high school and one year of college and want to keep up with it. After a week of study

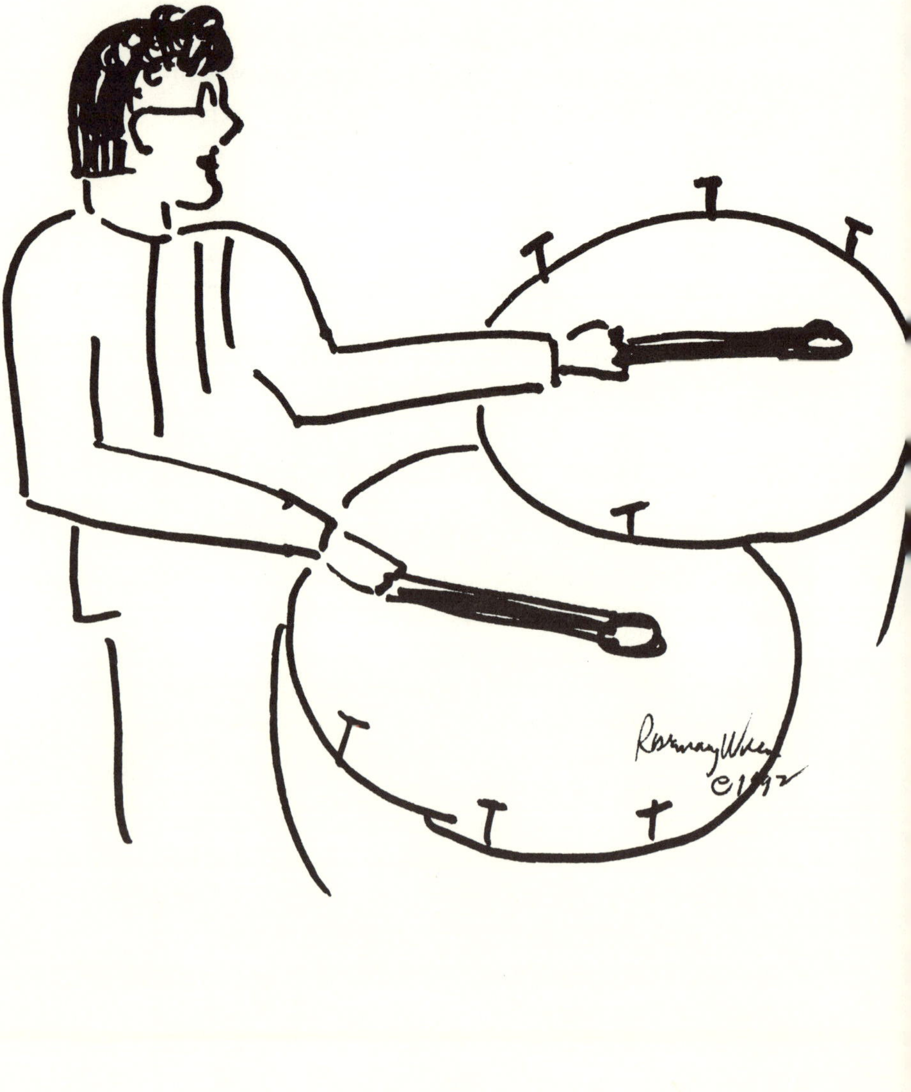

including two or three hours of homework every night, I look forward to making music."

The Pan Cultural Orchestra's programs are arranged to utilize and showcase the talent available in the school. The March concert featured Lyn Bronson, former DLI Russian student and local concert pianist, in the Chopin 2nd Piano Concerto. The DLI Vocal Ensemble sang songs of Chopin in Polish with soprano Sabra Hargrove; she is a member of the Air Force and a student of Arabic.

Gloria Gargiulo or one of the students directs the choral rehearsals and a language teacher helps with pronunciation. At the last Christmas concert the chorus sang carols in French, Italian, Spanish, Polish and Russian.

The orchestra plays light classics and folk music as well as the regular symphonic repertoire. Concerts in the past have ranged from Spanish Zarzuelas and French Can Can dances to Tchaikowsky, Mozart and Bach concerti. Thirty to forty people make up the group but it varies in size and nature because the DLI students come and go, graduate and leave the area. For this reason it was opened to the general community, to competent amateur and professional musicians. The only requirement is that you show up for Sunday rehearsals

once a week, play in the concerts, and practice! Small price for the joy of participating.

Pacific Magazine publisher Scott McClelland commends Ted for giving community musicians a chance to play. Scott studied cello as an adult after moving to the Peninsula and played with the orchestra for "two years of fun" until he broke his hand.

"Joyful! Very constructive, always new material, progressing and learning." This is violinist Walter Vicijan's description of the orchestra. Walter is an audio-visual technician for Asilomar Conference Center and has his own recording studio. He has played violin since the age five in Yugoslavia, then as a teenager with the Chicago Youth Symphony, now with the Pancultural for three years.

Through all the ups and downs and when the going gets rough during rehearsal Ted is patient and encouraging; Gloria sits quietly listening at every practice. Although Ted receives a small stipend, it is truly a labor of love for these two.

Community people involved in the orchestra include retired military percussionist Joe Gray, jazz bassist Ed Culver, flutist Kenny Stahl, composer Peter Evans, high school students, members of Monterey Youth Orchestra, homemakers, teachers, they all have this in common — they love to make music together.

✿ ✿ ✿

10. NOBODY SEEMS TO LISTEN

Today the American people will listen to psychologists and corporation presidents. The politicians lost credibility when they voted for the Gulf War, the biggest mistake since Thomas doubted Jesus. Most clergymen wave ambiguous flags — one side red, white and blue, the other side yellow like in coward. Historians point up the glories of ancient Mesopotamia and the complexity of the Arab tradition. Experts on the Middle East deplore the huge difference in our face toward Israel and our face toward Iraq. Diplomats ignore the conundrum of the prewar visits between Saddam and our ambassador.

Psychologists can tell us how to feel about all of the above and other things. How to explain to your children what we did in the war, why Daddy died there and how should you feel about it. At times of crisis the teams of psychologists are brought in: for children who see mass shootings either at school or on TV or to explain why Grandma lost it all at the Savings and Loan. The expert says it's OK to cry but no one will hold you until you get home to Mommy.

Psychologists have it and they are cleaning up. Early on in their careers they write a book — 'you're ok', 'compulsive eating', 'your inner child', 'holistic marketing', and most have a formula for success that applies to everyone. And these books pay off.

Carl Jung was one of the starters way back when, preaching the intellectualization of spirituality and the sterilization of emotion — the focus on dreams so that life is divorced from reality. His books are still paying off.

Psychiatrists and psychologists can tell the cancer victim's family how to cope with grief but not with the nagging question of whether their mother was killed by chemotherapy, radiation or cancer.

Doctors lost it when they began experimenting with humans instead of rats: chemotherapy that makes patients a lot sicker than they were before, with new misery that weakens the body so it can't fight. Radiation that destroys cancer cells but also destroys blood cells causing genetic effects. In Hiroshima radiation exposed victims showed increases in leukemia, thyroid cancer, and breast and lung cancer within the fifteen year period after the blast.

Does it make sense that an unusual cell revealed by a mammogram be immediately attacked by radiation or excised by deforming surgery? Do doctors consider that these abnormalities may *not* be dangerous or that the body has ways of healing itself? Radiation can make trouble that is not there. Cancer is a killer. So is radiation.

Many lawyers lose it when their focus constantly narrows to the dollar sign. Too often they are certain of special license to lie — not only in court but to their clients. Their game is ace manipulation and how to bring suit. At $200 to $300 an hour they will not tell you everything on the first visit.

Corporation presidents (CEOs) have a lot of credibility now especially if they 'get the job done'. American know how is still the best in the world, and anyone who can make the bottom line break the cash register has an audience. The job longevity may be somewhat precarious if the company starts to lose ground. Some CEOs have jumped off the bridge at this point. Others are offered cabinet posts or become director of the FDIC. However it is sometimes in reverse as in the case of General Schwarzkoph. Rumors say that many corporations are waiting to offer him the top. He definitely got the job done. Various renegades question the nature of the work but the public is eager to hear how he did it.

Above all the public wants to know how the company president spends all that money, $500 or 600 thousand a year, or even millions. It is difficult for the school teacher at $25 to 35 thousand a year to understand such luxury. This explains the popularity of TV's *Lifestyles of the Rich and Famous*.

Poets and artists are getting their jobs done. They are offering their work for inspection. But I do not see any *Lifestyles of poets and artists* on regular TV. I was refused a chance to read my poetry at one bookstore because I am not famous; they cater to psychiatrists and holistics who have best sellers. I just published by first book of poetry.

I have written poetry against the war and read it in public places. The flag I wave is also red, white and blue with a yellow lining — like in coward. In my defense I quote from E.B. White written during the second world war:

"In wartime the writer almost inevitably becomes propagandist and advocate, and although he may not realize it, he is operating against the grain, for the deepest instinct of a creative person is not to promote the world's cause but to keep the minutes of his own meeting."

But this was another war and another time. I must remember that now the world's cause is very much the minutes of my own meeting.

✿ ✿ ✿

© 1992

11. THE VIOLENT GLOVE

A professional boxer walking to the ring has a certain purity, the lonely innocence of a man facing death because he chooses it. Courage purges him clean, clear, chaste, romantic. His ascetic period of life before a bout creates a focus; he could be preparing for his first communion, his body learning the catechism of the perfect weight, the left hook and the right cross. He is the matador who crosses himself and kneels in prayer to face the bull.

That boxer is the purest thing in the fight business. His walk through paradise gate goes from barrio to spotlight, juvie hall to Ceasar's Palace, ghetto hunger to room service at the Marriott, coal mines to gold mines before the age of thirty. A whole series of fathers replace his own or the one he never had. The trainer tells him how to fight, the promoter when to fight, the manager where to fight, all taking their chunks of his paradise along the way.

That boxer is the purest thing in the fight business until his left jab shatters the enemy's jaw or his right cross smashes his opponent's brain to oblivion. There are a few instances when asking the help of God to maim, wound or destroy seems to be acceptable in our society. War and boxing have a lot in common.

However much one agrees with pacifism it is hard to reconcile Muhammad Ali's refusal to go to war with his acceptance of boxing as a career where the intent is violence against your brother.

Boxing is a sport? The dictionary defines 'sport'.

1. Any activity or experience that gives enjoyment or recreation; pastime, diversion.
2. Such an activity requiring more or less vigorous bodily exertion and carried on, sometimes as a profession, according to some traditional form or set of rules, whether indoors or outdoors.
3. fun or play
4. An object of ridicule; laughing stock; a person buffetted about as though a plaything.

None of the definitions say anything about violence and killing. Boxing in the final analysis can best be described by definition number 4: a boxer can be an object of ridicule especially if he loses. He definitely is a person buffetted about as though a plaything. Boxing promoters argue that players get killed in other sports such as football. The difference is: accidents do happen, but the *object* of other games is not to hurt, maim or kill. In boxing the aim is to hurt, destroy, *knock out* and the KO can easily lead to death or brain damage.

Thomas Hauser in *The Black Lights*(1) records that 439 deaths are documented in professional boxing since 1919. (Four of these happened in rounds thirteen to fifteen, meaning that the referee did not stop the fight early enough.)

Benny Paret, Duk Kuo Kim, Johnny Owen and Kiko Bejines all died of injuries inflicted on Worldwide TV in championship fights. They were injured on television for everyone to see.

Boxing causes brain damage. Muhammad Ali and Joe Frazier were never the same after their championship bout of 1971. "The Fight" put Frazier in the hospital for a long stay. Ali's loss was on points, but Frazier's left hook floored him in the fifteenth round, when both men were all ready battered. Brain damage may not manifest itself immediately.

Harry Carpenter, BBC-TV boxing reporter, wrote a love letter to the fight game in 1975 *Boxing, A Pictorial History.*(2) The text is pro boxing but the photos tell the story. Bloody broken faces, anguished eyes, stricken defeated heroes, a cloud of fear hanging over their glistening, perfect bodies. No more incriminating documentary against professional boxing could be made. Perhaps this was his subliminal intention?

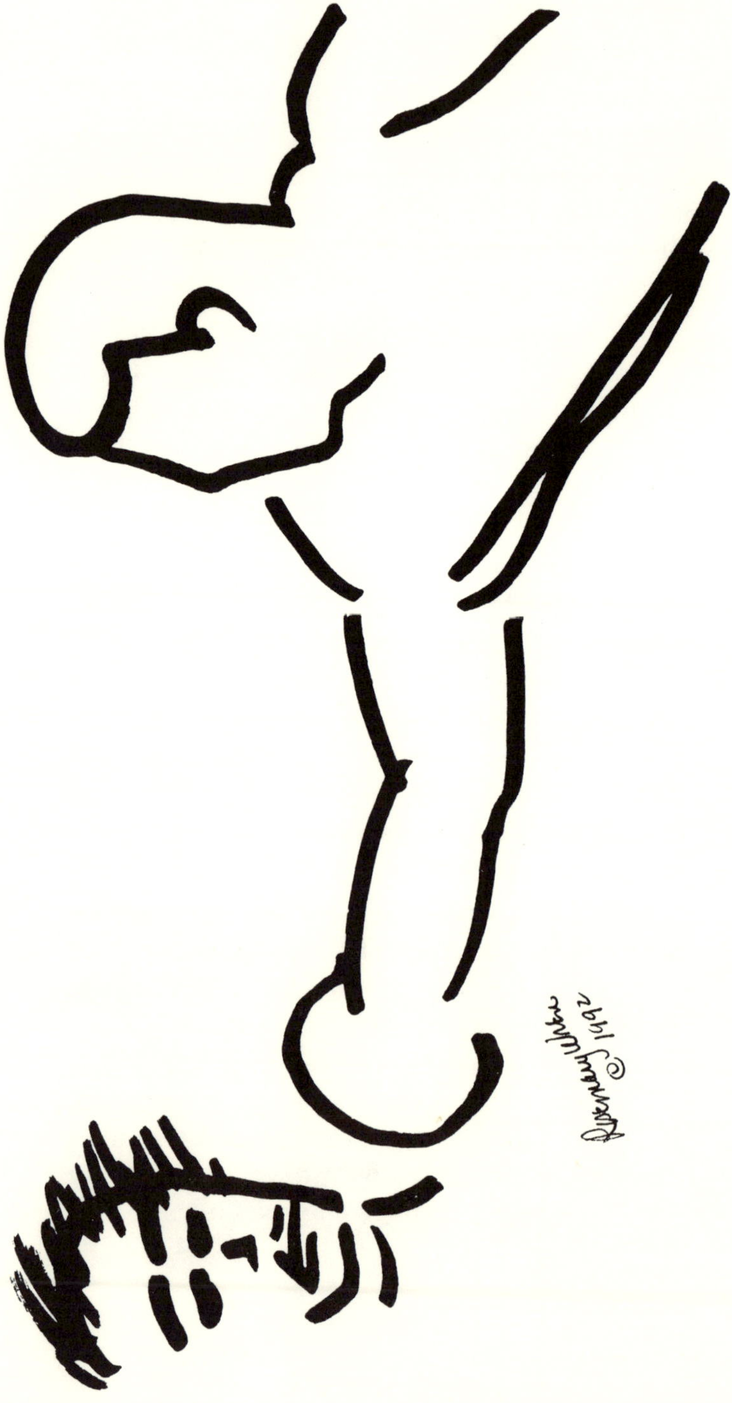

We are all guilty. We belong in jail with Mike Tyson. We stand back and condone a program which took a 'problem child', trained him for intense violence and focused his entire young life on the left hook, the right cross and especially the smash. In his first sixteen pro fights he KO'd twelve times in the first round.

This behavior brought him $60 million, a palatial estate and ten cars in the garage. Yet this 'behavior' can only be used in the ring and his inability to distinguish the acceptable use of power cost him his career. Heavyweight champion by the age of twenty Mike Tyson began in his teens, as a child, and had no time to grow up.

In 1971, three thousand year old frescoes were uncovered in Greece showing two boys in combat wearing boxing gloves on their right hands. Defenders of the fight game cite this as an example — historical longevity equals value. Professional boxing will never die, they say.

Successful pro boxers must be young. To the disadvantaged children of our country we hold out the violent glove. Is this all we have to offer?

✿ ✿ ✿

THE VIOLENT GLOVE

(1) Thomas Hauser THE BLACK LIGHTS
McGraw Hill 1986

(2) Harry Carpenter BOXING A PICTORIAL HISTORY
Henry Regnery Co. 1975

LET HISTORY REPEAT

Let history repeat
thou shalt not kill
the sentence is
psychiatric evaluation
incarceration, extermination

Let history repeat
thou shalt not destroy
unless in the ring
thousands watch
shout for killing
prize is millions
blows are aimed at the brain

Let history repeat
thou shalt not slay
unless in battle
thousands watch
shout for killing
prize is millions
blows will protect the sane

12. TURN LEFT AT THE BRIDGE

I think I have located the reason why there isn't more communion between UCSC and the town of Santa Cruz. It is because the citizens of Santa Cruz are afraid to go on campus and get lost.

It was 1981, a dark and stormy night. This is no exaggeration. If you lived in Santa Cruz in the Fall of '81 and Winter of '82, you added a new meaning to the word *rain*. Ever since that night the words *Thimann 3* strike terror to my heart. Always the interesting lectures I want to pick up at UCSC are at Thimann 3 (lecture hall), at night.

It was 1981, a dark and stormy night. I had just moved to Santa Cruz from San Francisco where I used to attend the theatre at night alone, drive the steepest hills in a car with a slipped clutch and always found a parking space downtown on the street. (I hate big garages.) But when it came to finding Thimann 3 at night, forget it. Once on campus the worst part was that if you found any stray students to ask directions, they didn't take Science. They were also afraid you might be faculty, if over thirty — perchance they gave the wrong turn on the grounds, it might incriminate them.

Once you make the right turn Thimann has

some very fascinating architecture at night. I have never seen it in the daytime.

I truly believe the Thimann Science Complex was set up as a maze for the citizens of Santa Cruz. In the wind and rain it was particularly dark and surrealistic save only for the large lighted library windows giving evidence of people who do take Science. I spent a lot of time looking in those windows knowing well they were not Thimann 3, afraid to knock on the windows for fear of upsetting a theorem. I also had a feeling if I entered the library I would just crawl under a table and go to sleep, being very tired of walking around in the rain, up and down the slippery steps.

Finally some people came along dressed in rain ponchos and rubber irrigation boots (hip length), carrying heavy voltage flash lights. They were discussing random molecular discovery so I knew they were the ones to follow. Sure enough three or four slippery staircases down we entered a warm, well-lighted space, Thimann 3 Lecture Hall. There were quite a few well groomed students who looked like they originated from Reaganomic households who could afford UCSC. Remember this was the early 80s.

There were also groups of scruffy bearded middle-aged men, serious in discussion among themselves. They could only be science faculty. There wasn't a bewildered housewife type like me in sight. (I had not yet entered my rebellious stage.) Nor did I see a triumphant look on any face that said, 'I came up the hill from Santa Cruz and two hours later found Thimann 3.'

The lecture/slides that night were wonderful — a discussion of Frank Lloyd Wright's *Hollyhock House* in Los Angeles by one of the curators from the LA County Museum of Art.

A few nights ago Thimann 3 came back in a rush. Another lecture called me up the hill to hear Jerry Nelson discuss the new Keck Telescope in Hawaii. This time I called the astronomy office for directions. They are good at tracking stars. 'Make a left as soon as you cross the bridge', said a young voice. She also said there would be students with flashlights telling where to park.

It was a dark night but not stormy. There were no students with flashlights. The road after the bridge led to a parking area where signs said, *Space reserved for Night Library.* I parked there anyway and began the exploration. It was exactly the same as ten years ago — I got lost. I gave up and went back to the car just as a couple drove up. Lucky night! It was a librarian who had worked at the University for twelve years. They allowed me to follow them through the maze. She said she still gets lost at UCSC, but not in that particular area.

Again the lecture was excellent and informative, presented by the originator of the Keck Telescope. I understand the largest telescope in the world (thirty-three feet span), because it uses thirty-six mirrors to determine the existence of certain stars. I use mirrors all the time to confirm existence. But getting lost has its proper humbling effect. I am going up the hill today to find Thimann 3 in the sunshine.

✿ ✿ ✿

13. THE WALNUT TREE

I guessed there was a reason for keeping that big old walnut tree which had such a wide wingspan, spreading over the roof of the garage.

During the long sad purple nights of my homeless weeks spent in the garage trying to sleep, as the raccoons and possums rolled walnuts over the roof, I dreamed of chopping the tree down — demolishing, cutting pale gray limbs, uprooting the graceful monument trunk. Walnut savoring animals would never disturb my sleep again.

That was a bad dream.

Instead an efficient tree man who listened to the tree as he trimmed and sawed, shaped the walnut tree away from the garage keeping strong magnificent arteries flowing. There remained leafing, shimmering buttery verdure, domed canopy, green covered walnuts. There was a bounteous crop. There was good argument for keeping the tree.

Now in winter when the harvest has been taken, the green umbrella fluttered down in windfalls, the silver branches curve bare against a dark rainy sky making long statements about reverence for life.

But the heart reason for this tree came on a shining February morning after the rain. As I trimmed rose bushes nearby a wild sweet melody cut the fragrant air, falling in sparkling drifts. A large red-bosomy robin perched high in the walnut tree was also caught by the sound. Although known as the 'herald of Spring,' this time he was not the singer. He sat enthralled as listener.

The robin and I were the audience for a small song sparrow singing out his heart much higher up. The robin and I were motionless for some time as pure joy swept down. The tree, the robin, the sparrow and I were united, inseparable, pulses together, life-current flowing, for part of a morning. The tree showed me its reason after the harvest, after the green umbrella had fluttered down, when its silver branches curved against the morning sky, only then could I see the robin, only then could I hear the sparrow.

A well known bird book published in the sixties says that poets give too much to these songs, that birdsongs do not have to do with Spring, happiness, joy of life; that birdsongs serve only to proclaim territory and attract the female. That may have been the sixties, but these are the nineties. The joyful cantata that affirms life and binds us together has been made.

✿ ✿ ✿

About the Author

Rosemary Wren, a resident of Santa Cruz, CA was born in Hawaii and grew up in Sacramento, CA. She is a graduate of San Jose State and San Francisco State Universities and is an artist/composer whose musicals have been produced in New York and Santa Cruz. Her first book of poems and paintings, *Rosemary's Calendar* was published in 1991.